Poker

The Math and Winning Strategy

By Mark Bresett

BONUS: DOWNLOAD MY <u>FREE</u> BOOK

Thank you for purchasing my book.

I would like to offer you a FREE book *25 Ways to Build Wealth: Reach Your Ultimate Goal With These Smart, Simple Steps.*

To get this 100% free book, visit my website:

www.Ways2BuildWealth.com/book

Best, Mark

Table of Contents

Introduction

Congratulations on purchasing *Poker: The Math and Winning Strategy* and thank you for doing so. Hundreds of thousands of dollars, if not more, change hands at poker tables worldwide each day. While a basic level of technical proficiency can help you keep a little of this money for yourself, if you ever hope to earn a serious payday then you will need to understand the math that the professionals use in order to keep themselves in the black in the long run.

To help you get to where you want to be, the following chapters will discuss a wide variety of topics that will help you take your game to the next level. First you will learn all about the ways in which math can be used in order to optimize your play to ensure you find success in the long term. Next, you will learn the importance of pot odds and how to maximize them in your favor. From there you will learn all about equity and how to put it to work for you.

Then you will learn all about expected value and how every raise, check, bet and call affects it in a meaningful way. With that out of the way you will learn about several different useful strategies that can be easily put into effect in virtually any hand. Next you will learn about the importance of hand combinatorics and how to determine them for both yourself and your opponent. Finally, you will learn how to find the best tournament for your skill level to put all that you have learned to the test.

There are plenty of books on this subject on the market, thanks again for choosing this one! Every effort was made to ensure it is full of as much useful information as possible, please enjoy!

Chapter 1
On Poker and Math

Poker is a game of skill where being able to read your opponent and the situations you find yourself in correctly will provide you with a significant improved chance of success whenever you sit down at a table. There is more to success than pure technical skill, however as mathematics and the ability to accurately determine the odds of success with a specific hand will give you a tremendous advantage when compared to those who purely operate on gut feelings.

A concrete understanding of the way that probability functions when you sit down to play a hand will naturally make it easier to make the right moves with each turn the game takes. While understanding probability won't guarantee you a 100 percent chance of success with every hand, following the odds will make certain that you win more than you lose overall.

The following chapters will discuss a wide variety of ways that numerous different equations can be applied to improve your play at all stages of the game, it is important to keep in mind that there is an inherent level of randomness to poker that not even the best players can eliminate entirely. From time to time you will be the victim of bad luck, plain and simple, but you will also benefit from it as well. The way you handle these losses is just as much a measure of your proficiency as a poker player as technical skill or correctly applying relevant equations. This mentality can be used to your advantage, as long as you have the equations to back it up in practice.

Probability basics

At its most basic, probability is the likelihood that a specific outcome will or will not occur. For example, a coin flip only ever has 2 outcomes, heads or tails. This then makes the probability of both outcomes 50 percent or 1 out of 2.

Unfortunately, a deck of cards has far more than 2 possible outcomes, which means determining the probability of certain cards aligning is much more complicated. Each deck has 52 cards, 4 suits and each suit has 13 different options (2-ace). This means that the probability of drawing a certain ranking of card is 1 out of 13, which is about 7.7 percent, and drawing a given suit is 25 percent. Furthermore, the odds of drawing a specific suit/ranking is about 1.9 percent.

To further complicate matters, a deck of cards has what is known as a memory. While each coin flip has an equal chance of coming up heads or tails, each card that is drawn from the deck changes the probability of all the remaining cards being drawn as well. For example, if you draw the ace of spades from the deck then the odds of drawing a second ace drops for 1 in 13 to 1 in 17 which drops the percentage of success from 7.7 percent to 5.8 percent.

Preflop probability: To continue with the ace example, if you were to determine the probability of getting a pair of pocket aces dealt to you preflop, you will simply need to multiply the probability of drawing one ace by the probability of drawing the second which equates to 7.7 percent multiplied by 5.8 percent which equates to 1/221 or .45 percent. To put this in context, if you paly 30 hands of Texas Hold'em in 1 hour then you can expect to start with this hand every 221 hands or once every 7.5 hours. The odds of receiving any pocket pair preflop are significantly better and work out to be 1 in 17 which, as we know, is 5.8 percent or about twice an hour.

Hand v. hand: This is perfectly fine if you are just drawing hands, but poker doesn't take place in a vacuum, which means it is vitally important to understand how your hand compares to that of your opponent if you hope to find success.

- In general, if you are holding a high pair and your opponent is holding 2 non-paired low cards then you have an 83 percent chance of winning.

- If you have a high pair and your opponent has a low pair then you have an 82 percent chance of winning.

- If you have a pair that is somewhat middling and your opponent is holding 1 low card and 1 high card then you have a 71 percent chance of winning.

- If you have 2 non-paired high cards and your opponent has 2 non-paired low cards then you have a 63 percent chance of winning.

- If you have 2 non-paired high cards and your opponent has a low pair then you have a 55 percent chance of winning.

Post-flop hand improvement

This is a list of the probabilities of several different common events and how likely they are to occur based on your starting hand.

- 32 percent chance 2 non-paired cards will match something on the flop.

- 6.5 percent chance a pair of suited cards will make a flush by the river.

- .85 percent chances that the same pair of suited cards will form a flush on the flop.

- 10.9 percent chance that a pair of suited cards will form 4/5s of a flush on the flop.

- 12 percent chance that a pair will match a set on the flop.

- .25 percent chance that a pair will result in 4 of a kind on the flop.

What this proves is that many poker players, even those who have a good deal of experience, tend to overvalue their starting hands, especially suited cards as they don't understand just how unlikely it is that these will ultimately result in a flush. What's more, lower quality pairs are frequently overvalued despite their low odds of turning into a set.

Outs: An out is any card that can improve your hand after the flop has occurred. A common scenario for players to find themselves in is holding 2 suited cards with 2 more suited cards appearing on the flop. When this occurs you would have a total of 9 outs, or remaining cards in the suit, that will turn your rubbish hand into something worth betting on.

While you can find long and complicated charts outlining the various probabilities of outs for basically any hand online. It is important to avoid these crutches and learn to work the details out for yourself. The easiest way to do so is through what is known as the rule of 4 and 2. This methodology works by first having you determine the number of cards that could appear which have the potential to give you a stronger hand before multiplying that number by 4 in order to come up with the approximate probability that a beneficial card will appear on either the river or the turn. If one of these cards doesn't materialize on the turn then you simply take the total number of potentially helpful cards and multiply by 2 to get a percentage explaining the likelihood that it will pop up on the river.

As an example, if you had the 4 flush as described above then you would have a 36 percent chance of hitting the fifth flush card on either the turn or the river (9 possible outs multiplied by 4 and an 18 percent chance to hit on the river if the turn card was a bust (9 multiplied by 2). This is always just going to be a rough estimate, however, as you never know what cards your opponent is holding which can skew things dramatically in certain situations. If you have reason to believe that your opponent is betting on the same hand you are going for then you would instead want to multiply by 7 (9-2) for a total of 28 percent and 14 percent respectively.

Decrease tilt: When used correctly and regularly, probability can make it easier to avoid emotional tilt while playing as long as you keep in mind that a high probability isn't the same as an automatic success. Unless you manage to create a scenario when you have a 100 percent chance of success, there is always a chance that the cards will fall against you and you will lose, even if you manage to put together 4 of a kind. As opposed to letting your emotions affect your gameplay, you will be far better off looking at each hand as an assorted combination of numbers. Sometimes these numbers will be in your favor and other times they won't, getting mad about it will only make you less likely to play well moving forward and skew the probability of success even more.

To help with this you may find it useful to keep in mind that playing to the probability will ensure that you find overall success in the long-term given a long enough timeline. If you always make the right moves then the probability of success is always going to be over 50 percent, which means that if you just tough out the rough patches you will generate a profit while playing eventually.

Chapter 2

Understanding Pot Odds

Understanding pot odds is crucial to maintaining a successful win/loss average at the higher levels of poker play no matter what your technical skills is like. This is, in fact, a critical concept that will determine the course of your poker career, regardless of how frequently you play and will affect your choices with each and every hand you play.

Figuring out the pots odds is as simple as keeping track of your likelihood of wining based on the hand you've been dealt and then using that information to determine if the right course of action is for you to bet, raise, call or fold with every single hand. As an example, if you currently have either a flush or a straight draw then you will be able to accurately decide if you are going to fold, call or raise based not only on the size of the bet but your overall odds of winning it as well. This can be a huge advantage in the long run as it means you don't need to throw money into pots that you automatically know aren't going to be worth it.

Determine the odds of the pot

There are 2 different ways to assess, the pot odds either through its percentages or through its ratios. While the ratio options is more frequently utilized in analysis of high-level play, percentages are often easier for those who are just getting started with the concept of pots odds to grasp. Regardless, the end result is going to work out to be the same, so which one you choose basically comes down to personal preference.

Determining pot odds via ratio: Even if you end up preferring to use the percentage method for your own purposes, knowing the ratio method will often make it easier for you to discuss pot odds with other poker players.

To utilize the principles at play here, let's move forward with the example of a 4 flush. In this example, you are holding the ace and 8 of hearts and the flop reveals the jack and 2 of hearts as well as the 7 of spades. This hand is a heads-up game with $80 in the pot and a $20 bet coming your way.

Start with the card odds: The first thing you need to do here is determine the odds of getting the cards you want via the rule of 4 and 2. With this done it becomes clear that you have a 36 percent chance to hit the flush on either the turn or the river and an 18 percent chance to hit it on the river if the turn doesn't go in your favor. To translate this into a ratio all you need to do is determine that there are still 47 cards in play and that 9 of them will give you the results you are looking for this means there are 38 cards that you don't want and 9 that you do. 38:9 can be reduced to 4:1.

Determine pot odds: Once you have the 4:1 ratio in mind you will then need to figure out what your odds of success are when compared to the odds of the pot. The odds of the pot can be determined by taking the ratio of the size of the pot compared to the size of the bet. As the bet is $20 to you on an existing $80 pot that means you need to call $20 to win a total of $100 so the ratio is 100:20, which can be simplified to 5:1.

Compare the results: The pot odds are 5:1 and the card odds are 4:1 which means that the potential for profit is great enough that it is worth taking the risk on hitting the flush. While this won't always be accurate, it is a good rule of thumb to ensure you only making profitable betting decisions in the long run.

Percentage method

To clarify the process used in the percentage method we'll take a look at a straight draw. For this example, you will be up against a single opponent on the big blind and you stayed in despite holding an unsuited 7 and 9 because no one rose preflop. You then lucked out and the flop revealed an ace, 8 and 6. You opponent then bests $30 into a $60 pot bringing the total to $90.

Find the card odds: Aside from the 4 and 2 method, to determine the odds for hitting the straight on the turn you can double the number of available outs which in this case is 8(4 10s and 4 5s) and then add 1 to the total to get a 17 percent chance of success.

Find the card odds: In order to stay in and see the river, you would need to bet $30 in order to win a total of $120. It is important to keep in mind that you will need to factor in the total of the pot, not just what you will win in profit if you take the hand. This is a crucial determining factor because the percentage

‿‿ 90 is very different when compared to 30 and 120. 30 is 25 percent of 120 so the pot odds are 25 percent.

When determining the odds it is important to always only take the next card you are going to see into account as every additional card is also going to mean an additional round of betting and factoring in hypothetical bets can skew the odds in unpredictable ways. In this instance, factoring in the odds for success from either the turn or the river would give you a nearly 40 percent chance of success, which would skew the results as you cannot factor in a hypothetical bet on the turn. This will ensure that you don't commit more money to the pot than is prudent given the state of things that you are sure about.

However, if you opponent goes all in on the flop then you would be able to factor in the results from both the turn and the river as you can guarantee that additional money will not be added to the pot before all the cards are shown which means the additional calculation would be accurate.

Determine the results: As you have already decided that you only have a 17 percent chance of success on the turn, then you would only want to bet if the cost to call was 17 percent of the pot or less. As this is not the case, it is smarter to fold rather than hold out for the potential completion of the straight. Just as with probability, there are charts you can easily access for this information, it is recommended that you learn the math yourself, however, as you will not always have easy access to charts, especially when you are playing live.

Making use of pot odds

Calling or betting: It is perfectly natural to have a hard time determining pot odds on the fly at first, just keep in mind that it will get easier with practice, especially as you get used to the ratios or percentages you see most frequently. The important thing is that if you base all of your decisions on this process then you will always come out ahead overall, regardless of which hands ultimately went on to work out in your favor.

Aside from maximizing the effectiveness of your calls, pot odds also come in handy when it comes to determining the right betting level to ascribe to when it comes to protecting your current hand. As an example, assume you have a strong indication that your opponent is currently working towards a flush. To force them to consider just how much they want to press the issue, you would then want to make a large enough bet to ensure the odds don't work in their favor when it comes time for them to call. In this scenario, it doesn't matter what your hand is, if your opponent calls against the odds then they will lose in the long run and if they fold you win the pot, which means you win either way.

Percentage and ratio differences: While the instances where you will need to mix percentages and ratios are few and far between, it is crucial that you understand the differences between the 2 when it comes to making comparisons using your preferred method. For example, 25 percent is not the same as a ratio of 4:1. 25 percent means that something is going to happen 1 out of 4 times, but a ratio of 4:1 is actually taking 5 total instances into account which means that every 5 times something happens 1 will work out in the desired way which is actually akin to 20 percent.

Implied odds

Implied odds are a natural extension of pot odds which can help you determine if it is in your best interest to call in the face of a surprise raise. Typically, the implied odds are going to tell you the amount you will win if the draw ends in your favor. If the amount you can expect to win is large, then the implied odds are going to be good and if this number is low then the implied odds will be small, or even nonexistent.

Pot odd and implied odd differences: Unlike when it comes to pot odds, there are no rules or formulas that can be applied to implied odds. Instead, calculating the implied odds is much more about understanding your situation and your opponent and then working out the situation based on experience. The more you play with the right analytical mindset, the more data you will have and your disposal which means the greater chance you will have of making the right decision when the time is right. Nevertheless, there are a few things that you can do in order to ensure you are on the right track.

Implied odds (positive): In this example, let's say you are the big blind and you were able to cost into the flop with a 6 and 7 unsuited. The flop is then kind to you and drops a king, 5, and 8 so you luck into an open ended straight draw. If your opponent bets then you can call or raise, confident that you have good implied odds to hit the straight and also to have the best hand in the round. This means you would want to be aggressively in hopes of maximizing the pot as much as possible. This betting is possible as the cards on the table would make it difficult for most opponents to determine the strength of your hand.

Implied odds (negative): In this example, let's say you are on the big blind and were able to limp into the flop with an unsuited 4, king. The flop then gives you the same general open straight draw with a 10, queen and jack. While the hand is more or less the same, the implied odds are much worse because there is little you can have with this hand besides a straight. This will make it much easier to stuff the pot as your opponent is going to assume you have the straight and bet accordingly. This assumption would then be confirmed if you bet on the turn as you did not bet on the flop or the preflop. While betting is still profitable as you are likely to win the hand, it is not as possible as it could have been.

Using implied odds: While it can be difficult to say just what you are going to win through the use of implied odds along, you will still be able to decide what you need to win in order to make calling a good use of your time and money. To do so, all you need to do is to find the odds of hitting your hand on the river and then subtracting that from the pot odds. This will provide you with the implied odds requirement and leave you with a new ratio that will make it easy to compare the call price to what the pot needs to be in order for this to work.

As an example, let's assume that you have a 4 flush that materializes on the flop before your opponent bets $10 into a $10 pot. This means you would be calling $10 to earn $20. The odds of this occurring are about 18 percent with odds of the pot set at 50 percent (10 into 20). The pot odds are dramatically not in your favor when compared to the hand odds so you would want to fold instead of calling the bet.

Implied odds effect: Implied odds are at their most useful when you can use them to decrease the overall severity of the pot odds in many situations. If you have a feeling that you can squeeze more money out of your opponent via multiple betting rounds as opposed to one large play then the initial call will still make sense even if the pots odds aren't as strong as you might like.

For example, let's assume that you have a nuts draw in the form of a straight. The odds of hitting the fifth card on the turn are approximately 5 to 1. If your opponent then places a $25 bet into a $100 pot, then you have 4 to 1 that this will work out in your favor. Assuming your straight is still somewhat vague, then the implied odds are still generally strong assuming the straight you are working with isn't clearly giving away your position. This is then the right choice as you have a greater chance of making money as opposed to folding.

Chapter 3
All About Equity

Equity is an important concept for every poker player to understand as it makes it easier to determine the right course of action based on your current hand and can make it easier to determine if you want to bet or check based on extraneous variables. When playing poker, the equity of your hand can be thought of in terms of how much of an individual pot belongs to you based on the odds that you are going to take it at various points during the hand. For example, if your hand is good, but not great, and you currently have a 60 percent chance to win then you currently have 60 percent of the available equity as well.

For example, let's assume you have the king and ace of diamonds in hand preflop and you know for a fact your opponent has the jack of hearts and the 10 of spades and there is $30 in the pot. If this is the case then you have a 65 percent chance of winning the hand, which means you have $19.50 worth of equity (65 percent of $30).

Equity doesn't stay the same for the entire hand; it changes with each new card that is shown. This means that if the above is still true and the flop shows the 10 of clubs, 2 of hearts and jack of diamonds then your chance of winning plummets to 22 percent, which gives you equity of $6.60. Then, when the turn produces the queen of spades you suddenly have a straight and your equity increases to 91 percent or $27.30. Meanwhile your opponent only has 9 percent equity and will only take the pot if they catch a jack or 10 on the river.

Maximizing equity

While having an understanding of the portion of the pot you currently control is useful, it is rarely possible to determine the exact amount of equity you have at a specific time unless you and your opponent are both all in and have revealed your cards. Nevertheless, it is still in your best interest to work to determine the current level of equity as it makes it easier to ensure you are making the right moves in the moment. If your assumed equity means you have the best hand at the table then you are going to want to bet for value in order to sweeten the pot as much as possible.

Bet for value: In the above example, you had walked into a straight on the turn, which left you with 91 percent equity. What this means is that for every extra dollar you can get into the pot, you are most likely going to earn 91 cents. With this in mind it makes the most sense to try and force your opponent to dump as much money into the pot as quickly as possible. As such, with this in mind you would want to bet in such a way that it maximizes the amount of money you can potentially win from the hand. This is always going to be the correct play as long as you have 51 percent equity or greater.

While it is possible that your opponent could still catch the 10 or jack they need on the river, this should not factor into your decision as it is impossible to tell the future and thus not worth factoring into your decisions, equity is all about the moment and the moment says you should bet. While this does mean you are enhancing what you might lose if you end up being outdrawn, with equity in your favor it makes more sense to be aggressive as opposed to defensive. By pumping as much money into the pot when equity is in your favor you maximize your long-term profit potential.

Equity also explains why it makes sense to raise preflop if it seems likely you have the best hand and also verifies the logic behind being the aggressor, working to reduce the total number of players and buying position. Not only should equity an important part of your strategy, it also makes it make sense to raise the stakes for additional rounds of betting which will compound your advantage assuming your equity is maintained.

Drawing hands and equity

As a general rule, if you are holding the best possible cards at one stage of the hand then you are more likely to emerge victorious with the pot when all is said and done. Even so, sometimes it is also possible to move forward with an unmade hand as if it were a draw and still have the highest chance for overall victory. In this scenario, your pot equity will still be rather high which means it will still make sense to bet as though your hand were already complete.

As an example, assume you have in your hand the jack of diamonds and the queen of diamonds and the flop provides you with the 4 of clubs, and the 9 and 10 of diamonds. If your opponent starts off with a very strong bet then it is safe to assume that you are not holding the overall strongest hand. However, you would still have equity of about 52 percent assuming your opponent isn't holding anything better than 2 pair. The only hand that would have a greater equity than yours would be a set and, even then, the difference would just be marginal. This is the case because you have a wide variety of outs with this hand, including those that can make a flush as well as a straight. In this instance, it still makes sense to bet for value because the odds of ending up with a win are quite large.

Equity in multiplayer scenarios: For this example, you will assume that you have the same hand as before, the second player holds the 4 of diamonds and the 9 of spades and a third player has stuck around with the 10 of hearts and the 10 of clubs. In this scenario, you are no longer in the dominant position. You would be knocked down to around 45 percent equity while the player with the pair has about 54 percent and the remaining player picks up the last 1 percent.

If this were a heads-up scenario, and you had 45 percent equity then you would need to check and then fold assuming the other player placed another bet, but the third player makes things a bit less cut and dry. If things continue along these lines and neither of the other players fold then each player has generated

33 percent of the pot. As 33 percent is less than 45 percent it means that for every 33 cents you put into the pot you get 45 cents back when means you are going to want to continue stuffing the pot as much as possible. The fact that you aren't quite favored to win is irrelevant in this case as the numbers work out and mean you will ultimately turn a profit in the long run.

This is not the case, then, if the weaker player folds without putting anything more into the pot. This would change the contribution percentage to 50 percent instead of 33 percent which means for every 50 cents you put in you can only count on getting 45 cents back which is a losing proposition which means you would want to fold after the next bet or raise to protect yourself from loss. As a general rule, it will always make more sense to invest in pots whose equity exceeds the percentage of the pot you are responsible for and fold when the percentage is not in your favor.

Chapter 4

Find the Expected Value

In every game of poker, each raise, check, bet, call and fold all have a unique expected value. More specifically, some will lead to a profit while others will result in a loss and, of those that generate a profit, some will ultimately generate more of a profit than others. It stands to reason then, that the goal of every action you take should be to generate the largest amount of expected value (EV) overall.

Positive expectation value (+EV) is the term used for plays that are likely to generate a profit both in the long-term and in the short-term. Negative expectation value (-EV) is the term used for plays that are likely to result in a loss sooner or later. It stands to reason, then, that your goal will need to be to maximize the former and minimize the later as much as you possibly can.

Determine EV

In order to determine the EV of a given action all you need to do is to multiply the results of all of the possible outcomes by the probability that each one has to actually occur and then add all of these results together. While it sounds complicated, it is no more difficult than the other equations discussed in the previous chapters, it just contains a larger amount of numbers.

To illustrate, let's say that your friend tells you that you can play a game where every time a coin is flipped and comes up tails you have to pay them $1 but if it comes up heads they pay you $1.50. In order to decide if you should play or not you would start by determining the probability of each action occurring, which is 50 percent assuming they are not using a loaded coin. The equation would look like this:

Heads = -$1

p(heads) = .5

Tails = $1.50

p(tails) = .5

From there, you would then want to multiply each outcome by its probability before adding the results together in order to determine the true EV of each flip of the coin. In so doing you would then determine that the average you would make on each flip is $0.25. Put another way, for each 2-coin flips you are likely to make a 50-cent profit, which would then be divided in 2 for a total profit of 25 cents, each time the coin is flipped. It doesn't matter if it ends up being heads or tails 10 times in a row or 100 times, given a long enough timeframe it will equal out to 25 cents per toss.

Poker example: Taking the example back into the poker arena, let's say you are sitting on a 4 flush after the turn with 2 spades on the board and 2 in your hand. Furthermore, assume to pot is currently worth $100 and your opponent just finished raising you $50 which means that for $50 you have the chance to win $150.

All you need to do is determine if it is worth your while to call based on how likely you are to make your flush on the river.

You will be able to get most of the way to the correct answer with pot odds, but you can determine the exact amount you will win or lose thanks to EV, which can tell you what the average profit you will make assuming you call the bet. The equation would look like this:

Call, hit flush = +$150

P(hit flush) = 0.2

Call, miss flush = -$50

p(miss flush) = 0.8

The probability that you will connect on the river is going to be about 20 percent, which means the probability is .2. This means that your odds of failure are .8 or 80 percent. You will also need to be aware of the disparity between the potential $150 profit and the guaranteed required bet of $50. Money used to get to this point in the game isn't factored in separately as it is already gone. .2 multiplied by $150 is $30 and .8 multiplied by -$50 is -$40, which means that each type you place this bet on the hopes that you hit the flush you are actually costing yourself $10.

As such, the decision to make the bet can be thought of as an -EV play, which means you should avoid it at all costs. This is not to say that you won't be successful 20 percent of the time, it only says that this is a losing value proposition in the long term which means you should avoid it to ensure you poker career is profitable overall.

Using expected value

Every single move you make in a given hand should be done with an eye towards maximizing your expected value in order to improve your long-term chance of success. This is often easier said than done, however, as it can be difficult to work out the EV of all the options open to you in real time in the midst of an actual game.

If you find that this is the case, you will often need to rely on your post play analysis to determine what you should have done in situations where what you did do ended up clearly being the less than optimal play. With practice, and plenty of after the fact consultation, you will find that over time it will become easier and easier to make the right play with confidence in the moment without worrying about determining the exact EV of every move. It is more important to know what the right move is and to make it then to know exactly how profitable the right move is as long as you make the right moves when it matters most.

EV and equity

It can be easy to confuse EV with equity as they both concern the odds that a specific move is the correct choice in a given situation based on the overall potential for profit. While they are similar, and can even work together frequently, they do have some differences that should help you keep them straight.

First things first, equity is a percentage that can be used to tell you how likely you are to win a given hand while EV will tell you how much profit or loss you can expect from a given action. Equity is essentially the raw data that will point you in a given direction while EV focuses more on the numbers at work on the table. If you take the time to consider the equity of a hand and find out how much money you have the potential to win or lose then you wind up with EV.

When variance comes to call

To understand why this is the case, it is important to understand how variance factors in to every hand that you play. At its most basic, variance is the term that is used to describe the downswings and upswings that come along with prolonged poker play. It is also a useful way to describe the difference between the amount of profit you can hope to win on average after a night at the table in the long term as well as the short term. For example, if you average a profit of $500 per month that you play poker, then sometimes you are going to lose $1,500 in a month and other times you are going to win $2,500 but when it is all taken together $500 is the average. As long as you stick to +EV moves your total is going to balance out to $500 per month with a long enough timeline.

While there is undeniably a high skill ceiling when it comes to playing poker successfully, there is no player who is so skilled as to avoid variance entirely. You fundamentally never have control over the cards you are dealt or the ones that come up on the table. With that being said, the following factors can alter the amount of variance you experience by a fair amount.

Play style: If you favor an aggressive or loose style of play, then you are naturally going to end up playing far more hands than someone who plays a tight and cautious game. You will naturally open yourself up to a greater degree of variance if this is the case, both because you are playing far more hands and because you are playing lower quality hands as well. If you are trying to minimize the amount of variance you experience, tighten up your game.

Game type: If you are looking for a low variance game that is similar to the currently most popular type of poker which is Texas Hold'em, then you may want to consider playing Omaha instead. Each player receives more cards overall when playing Omaha which means that the variance that each individual card introduces to the game is lessened as well. In fact, when a player goes all in with an Omaha hand, the edges are lessened and, as a result, every hand has about a 15 percent greater chance of success than if that player made the same move with the same hand during a game of Hold'em. The lessened edges mean that variance has less of an opportunity to intervene.

Betting type: Limit games naturally have a lower overall amount of variance simply because the amount that a single player can add to the pot at any given time is significantly decreased. The less money that is flowing through a table, the less that variance can affect it, simple as that.

Game type: The variance in SNGs is going to be less than that found in MTTS as the odds that you are going to come out on top are much more in your favor with the former than the latter. This is balanced out in the grand scheme of things as the payout is also going to be much smaller with SNGs than it is with MTTs.

Personal variance: It is crucial to your long term success that you learn to take notice of how much variance is currently affecting you at any given time so that you can filter it out before determining your current level of success at a given table. Variance has a way of draining off the willpower of the best players if they let it influence them as to the current overall quality of their play. It can cause them to start seconding guessing their next moves, simply because it looks like the moves they are making are the wrong ones, even if they are actually playing perfectly. It is not without merit, however, as variance is also the reason that bad players keep playing, because every now and then it makes them feel as though they are the best players in the world.

In order to determine how much variance you are currently dealing with, you will want to keep track of your hand equity, EV plays and your overall results as this will give you concrete examples to hold up to the variance you are experiencing in the moment. This will help you keep a clear head and make it easier to realize when you are playing a completely competent long game despite the fact that your short-term results are less than ideal.

Having the confidence to believe in yourself is supremely important when it comes to seeing a period of unlucky variance through to completion. After all, things will never turn around if you quit playing so all you can do is keep making the right choices in the moment and let the negative variance straighten itself out. Learn to trust yourself and the choices you make in the short term and the results will take care of themselves.

Chapter 5
Useful Strategies

Cbet

Also known as the continuation bet, the cbet is a strategy that is extremely popular these days. This is because it is extremely effective while also fairly easy to pull off when done correctly. A cbet is simply a bet that is made on the flop by a player who raised preflop, regardless of whether or not the flop actually improved their hand.

This means that if you raised preflop because you were holding the king of hearts and the ace of spades, you would want to bet again, even if the flop dropped a 9 of clubs, 4 of diamonds and the queen of hearts. Doing so will provide you with the ability to win the pot via a bluff by making the other players assume that your hand is better than it actually is. This play succeeds because, statistically speaking, your opponent is only going to match a pair on the flop some 33 percent of the time. This, in turn, means that the more you dump into the pot early on, the less likely the pot odds are actually going to work out in your opponent's favor, even if they have the better hand.

Sizing a cbet: The most effective cbets are going to be somewhere between three-fourths and 2-thirds the size of the pot, depending on the read you have on your opponent. If the bet you place is too low then your opponent has the option to call because the pot odds are still in their favor if they have the better hand. Meanwhile, if it is too high then they will be equally likely to fold but you run the risk of over-committing if they aren't fooled by your bluff and continue to move forward with the hand.

Reading your opponent: The level of skill of the player you are attempting to bluff is going to play a big part as to whether or not you will want to run this strategy. The greater their skill level, the less likely you will be able to pull off the cbet. Additionally, seasoned players are going to be more likely to see through the play as it happens regularly, and novice players are going to be more likely to stumble through and call, even if the pot odds are against them. As a general rule, you can expect to catch a serious player with this bluff once or twice in a game before it stops working so make sure you take full advantage of these instances.

Double barrel

If you make a cbet on the flop and it doesn't go as planned so someone calls your bluff, you will often find that the best course of action is to double down and make another cbet on the turn. This is known as the double barrel and it is important to think before you act because at this point you are stuffing a pot whose odds are almost always going to be against you.

When you make this play it is important to have a clear read on your opponent and make sure that they are not just a calling station as if this is the case then it is unlikely that they will change their mind, no matter how much you throw into the pot. The best chance for success with this strategy comes when you have an opponent who you know already prefers to float a large number of flops. Another good time to go all in on this strategy is when you are facing an opponent who has shown that they prefer to avoid head-to-head showdown scenarios.

Even though this is a strategy based around bluffing, it is always a good idea to go after the double barrel only when you have a halfway decent hand or one that you can draw into on the river. This is because there is always a chance that your opponent doesn't fold which leaves you on the hook for a fatter than average pot. The best time to use this strategy in a way that leaves you somewhat protected is when you are holding a pair of overcards to start that matched a pair on either the flop or the turn.

The most effective double barrels are those that occur when the turn shows an onvercard, which generates an easy narrative for your opponent to follow, which says that you hand is a good deal more powerful than it actually is. Assuming your opponent calls the first cbet then it is reasonable to assume they have a medium or top pair or better which the overcard on the turn then throws completely out of whack, dropping their equity in the process. This, followed by the second aggressive bet, makes it easy for them to reconsider before calling the second bet, especially as the increased pot means the odds will likely not be in their favor.

Alternately, if the turn shows a low card or a card that matches something from the flop then the equity is almost always going to be against you and it will typically be a better choice to fold rather than waste even more money through a bet that your opponent is far more likely to call. This scenario will have either strengthened your opponent's hand or given them reason to assume that your hand was not strengthened either, both of which are reason enough for them to call a second time.

If the turn card is somewhere in the middle of the road, that is, creating no match with the flop or your hand and coming up not as the top pair then the decision your opponent is going to make will be decided by their opening hand. This means that you will only want to double barrel with an average turn card if you think your opponent's range is low.

3bet

When used correctly a 3bet is most effective in games between $50NL and $200NL. A 3bet play can occur preflop as someone bets and then someone else raises. The 3bet occurs when a third player raises on top of the existing raise. This will cause many players to automatically assume that the third player has a fantastic hand, typically pocket queens or better. 3betting light is similar except that the hand you attempt it with isn't as good as the hand you have during a regular 3bet, and is typically something like a suited mid-range connector. While it is dangerous if you use it without the cards to back it up, it is still almost always a +EV move.

The 3bet is effective in part because of how common cbets have become in recent years. Even if you have a strong hand, calling a raise preflop typically leaves you at a disadvantage because it typically negatively affects your pot odds and gives your opponent initiative for the remainder of the hand. Typically, you will have little option but to fold or to hit something on the flop and fold if you don't. However if, instead of calling, you 3bet, then loose players will be put into an -EV scenario as it makes it seem like your opening range is quite extreme while at the same time giving you the initiative for the rest of the hand.

The best time to 3bet light is when you are in position on LP as raisers who are on EP are typically going to end up with a stronger hand. The most effective time to 3bet light is against those players who are aggressive and semi-tight or aggressive and very tight. Ideally you will find yourself in a scenario where an aggressive and tight player raises when you are in the CO or on the button.

Most importantly, you are going to want to avoid a light 3bet if you are playing with players who have proven that they are only going to raise when they have very strong hands. This means that you are unlikely to win if they don't fold and also they are unlikely to fold and will likely see the play through to the end. On the other hand, you are also going to want to avoid the play against extremely loose players, as they are more likely to call regardless of the actual strength of their hands.

Finally, you are going to want to avoid making a light 3bet with lower tier Broadway hands like king-queen, king-jack, and jack-queen along with weaker aces like ace-jack and lower. These types of hands are easily dominated and if your opponent calls then you are going to be in a much worse position than you would be with a somewhat stronger hand. The best course of action if you have a hand in this range is to call. If you do 3bet and end up moving forward and then missing the flop completely you are going to want to follow it up with a cbet that is two-thirds the size of the pot to keep the bluff going in a reliable manner.

Chapter 6
Hand Combinatorics

Combinatorics is the fancy name given to the process used to determine the number of potential combinations of a given hand that exist based on the situation. For example, it is how you answer the question: "How many different ways you can be dealt a pair of queens." Combinatorics is useful as it makes working out these types of specifics quick and relatively simple once you learn how it's done. This, in turn, makes it easier for you to make the most profitable decision in the moment based on the probability that certain hands will appear.

Hand Combinations

If you were to manually break down a preflop ace-king hand by writing out all of the ways you could receive it, including king of clubs, ace of clubs, king of spades, aces of spades, ace of hearts, king of spades, etc. you would eventually end up with a total of 16 different variations. Alternately, if you wanted to determine how likely it would be to get a specific pocket pair you would come up with just 6 variations. While this shows that you are nearly 3 times as likely to find a non-paired hand compared to a pocket pair, combinatorics is good for much more than that. For the record, there are 1,326 different possible preflop hand combinations in total.

Utilizing known cards: Being able to determine the specifics for various combinations in the moment is a crucial part of utilizing this strategy successfully. For example, let's assume that you are currently holding an unsuited queen and king preflop and then see a 4, 10 and king revealed on the flop. In this scenario, you would need to determine how many king, pocket 10 and ace combinations there are so you know what your opponent might be holding to determine if you are currently the majority equity holder. To find this number you would make use of the equation $C=A_1 + A_2$. C is the complete number of relevant combinations, A1 is the total number of cards available that the first card could be and A2 is the remaining number of cards that the second card could be.

To determine these amounts, all you need to do is to multiply the number of available first cards by the number of available second cards. To determine the numbers in the example cited above, you would need to come to the conclusion that there are 4 available aces and 2 unaccounted for kings which, when multiplied means that there are 8 possible ace-king combinations floating in the ether.

From here you would then want to figure out the potential pairs that your opponent could be holding and to do so you would use the equation $C=[A \times (A-1)]/2$. C is the number of possible combinations total and A is the number of cards that are still available. To figure out the specifics you would take the number of cards that are available and multiply that by the number of cards available minus 1 and divide the results by 2.

In the previous example, if you wanted to determine how likely your opponent was to have pocket 10s then you would start with the number of 10s floating unaccounted for which is 3. This means the equation would work out to [3 x (3-1)]/2 or 3 total.

Putting combinatorics to use: When it comes to using combinatorics in play, they are useful when it comes to determine a player's range, which makes it easier to determine the hands they are likely to play over time. As an example, if you have already decided that your opponent is 3betting with a tight range then you can assume that they will only ever bet if they have the best hands so you can then use combinatorics to determine the likelihood that they are holding pocket aces, pocket kings or a suited ace-king.

While, at face value, it may seem as though this 3betting player is only ever betting on pocket pairs, the proper utilization of combinatorics can expand your assumptions dramatically. When taken at face value the likelihood of each hand in 33 percent with the pocket pair combining to be a 66 percent chance. However, if you take combinatorics into account then you will realize there are 6 different possible ace-king combinations that can result in pocket pairs but 16 different ace-king combinations in total. This skews the data so that the other player is only likely to play a pocket pair 21.5 percent of the time and an ace-king hand 57 percent of the time.

While you won't always be able to act on the information that you determine, especially if your hand is less than ideal, it does show how effective it can be in order to understand the hands your opponent is likely to play in a given situation. This same method generally applies if you are looking to determine the probability range of hands that could be a threat based on the current flop by simply breaking down the numbers behind each relevant hand combination. This will make it easier for you to determine specifics such as if your opponent is more likely to be angling towards a set or a straight draw.

As an example, let's say that you have a pocket pair of 6s in hand and the jack of hearts, ace of spades, 8 and 6 of diamonds and the 2 of clubs on the table. Assume that the pot is currently sitting at $12 and you have already committed $10 before your opponent went all in for a total of $60. You would then need to call for $50 in order to make a profit of $72. Assume you also know that your opponent either has a set that includes an ace or 2 pair with an ace in hand.

To determine the right course of action, the first thing you would need to do is determine the pot odds which tell you that you would want at least a 38 percent chance of making the wining hand for it to be the right choice for you to call. With this in mind, you would then use combinatorics to decide if calling is the right choice based on the details you have available to you. In order to determine the right move you would need to figure out the number of different combinations you can currently beat as well as those you are likely to lose to.

Hands you win against

AJ=3x3=9

A8=3x3=9

A6=3x1= 3

A2=3x3=9

22=(3 x 2)/2 =3

Hands you lose to

AA=(3x2)/2=3

JJ=(3x2)/2=3

88=(3x2 /2=3

Once you add everything together you will find that you have a good chance of winning against 33 different hands (79 percent) as opposed to losing to just 9 hand combinations (21 percent). As you already know you are only looking for 36 percent equity minimum in order to move forward, which means that doing so in this situation makes sense.

This is an important point to keep in mind because without the help of combinatorics it could easily have seemed that the split was going to be closer to 50/50 which would have changed the call from +EV to -EV. The fact that the actual results are closer to 80/20 in your favor makes it firmly a +EV move. Being able to determine the range your opponent is working in is helpful, understanding the individual likelihood of all the hands in a given range is vital.

Chapter 7
Poker Tournaments

The first thing you are going to need to do before determining the right poker tournament to enter is figure out a few things about yourself and the kind of tournaments you should be the most interested in. First, you will need to consider the kind of player you are. There are 3 broad categories for players and honestly assessing yourself is the key to finding the right tournament for you. While it may be tempting to overestimate your skills, the only person you will be hurting by doing so is yourself.

Amateur: If you mostly play for fun then you are likely looking for a tournament that is full of other amateur players. This doesn't mean you are a bad player who loses a lot, it just means that you mostly play poker in a causal way. If you don't have a tournament bankroll set aside or don't want to worry about proper bankroll management, then you are going to want to look for tournaments that have a low fixed buy-in, offer a decent shot at ending in the money and provide some excitement as well.

Expert: If you play in a lot of ring games online and tend to regularly win a fair amount of money then you probably fall into this category. This means you likely play in tournaments occasionally, but rarely do so on the regular. You will want to look for tournaments that offer a large cash prize or have a field of players who have a lower skillset that you can take advantage of.

Tournament players: If you have a separate tournament bankroll aside from your standard cash play bankroll and play in tournaments on the regular then you are this type of player. Odds are you already have a list of places to play in tournaments and are just looking for some additional options.

Picking the right tournament

Determine the field size: The first thing you are going to want to determine before you start looking at specific tournaments is how many players you are interested in playing against. The options range from dozens to thousands so there are plenty of options to choose from. The name of the game in tournament play is skilled players taking advantage of less-skilled players, which means that the more players in a game the greater your return on investment if you have the skills to back it up.

On the contrary, however, while smaller tournaments mean you have greater odds of running into other skilled players, they also mean you are going to have to deal with less variance overall. The larger the tournament, the greater the chance that something will go wrong and that you will walk away with nothing, the smaller the tournament the greater your chance to rely on your own skill. Additionally, if you are just getting your feet wet in tournament play you will want to consider smaller tournaments as they will give you a better chance to test your skill and improve your tournament play for the future.

Consider the buy-in: If you don't already have a tournament bankroll and aren't terrible interested in mastering bankroll management before you start playing in tournaments, then all you need to do is to look for tournaments with a buy-in level that you are comfortable losing if things don't go according to plan. Additionally, you will want to keep in mind that the higher the buy-in the greater the odds are that you will be playing against skilled players. Choosing a buy-in level that you are comfortable with is key to ensuring that you mind is on the poker you are playing, not the fact that you could end up losing more than you can afford to. This will ensure that you are not distracted, especially if you make it to the final table and the money is really on the line.

Consider what level of play you are looking for: In general, the bigger the potential payout, the greater the overall skill level of the players you are up against is going to be. This isn't always a hard and fast rule, however, as tournaments that have a lot of publicity also often get a large number of players who are playing just to say they were there. The best example of this is the World Series of Poker, which always includes hundreds of players who are competing just because they can. This is where tournament specific research comes into play as if you are a skilled player you can likely make a profit without having to duke it out at the final table.

Consider the blinds: The blind structure of the tournament is going to determine the number of chips you start with in comparison to the starting blinds and also how quickly those blinds are going to increase in value. If you are just getting started playing in tournaments then it is best you look for a high chip to blind ratio to ensure the blinds increase slowly as this will ensure you get the most out of your initial buy-in. This type of shallow structure will ensure that you are more likely to last at least a few rounds as long as your skill level is somewhat above 0.

For players who are more skilled, they are going to want to think long and hard about the strengths of their game and then look for a structure that plays to their strengths or at least minimizes their weaknesses. If you play a lot of ring games then you will want to go for tournaments that start with deep stacks so that the tournament plays out like the games they are used to. If you play in tournaments regularly then the shallow stack tournament might be a nice diversion or a tight stack game might give you a challenge.

Consider the prize structure: The prize structure that is right for you is, by and large, going to come down to personal preference. The first thing you are going to want to consider is the cut that the house is going to take. Tournaments will small stakes typically take a 10 percent cut for the house. If you are buying in to a tournament for more than $100 then the cut will decrease somewhat. If it is a tournament with few players and low stakes then the house might take as much as 20 percent of the total pool. These tournaments are typically some of the hardest to profit from as there is very little profit to be made to start with.

Conclusion

Thank you for making it through to the end of *Poker: The Math and Winning Strategy*, let's hope it was informative and able to provide you with all of the tools you need to achieve your goals, whatever it is that they may be. Just because you've finished this book doesn't mean there is nothing left to learn on the topic, expanding your horizons is the only way to find the mastery you seek.

Additionally, it is important to keep in mind that many of the theories and strategies outlined in the previous chapters require a fair bit of in the moment mental math which means that you are likely going to want to practice with them before attempting to utilize what you have learned when there is lots of money at stake. Furthermore, as games played without any real stakes don't allow you to practice a correct mindset, it is recommended that you practice in very low stakes games so money is still on the line and you can practice in a live environment without quite as much risk as you would come up against in a real game.

If you initially have a hard time using these formulas in the moment, it is important to not lose hope and keep trying to work them out with each hand you play. Mastering the skills you need to understand the math behind poker is a marathon, not a sprint, slow and steady wins the race. Practice, practice, practice and eventually you will find that the numbers you need manifest themselves without you even having to think about it.

Finally, if you found this book useful in anyway, a review on Amazon is always appreciated!

24112383R00032

Printed in Great Britain
by Amazon